WELCOME TO THE WORLD OF
Skunks

Diane Swanson

Whitecap Books
Vancouver / Toronto

Dedicated to Jeffrey Warren

Edited by Elizabeth McLean
Cover design by Steve Penner
Cover photograph by Thomas Kitchin/First Light
Interior design by Margaret Ng
Typeset by Susan Greenshields
Photo credits: Wayne Lynch iv, 4; Erwin and Peggy Bauer/First Light 2;
John H. Hoffman/Arizona-Sonora Desert Museum 6; Thomas Kitchin 8, 12, 18,
26; Bill Silliker Jr. 10; Daniel J. Cox/Natural Exposures 14, 24; Thomas
Kitchin/First Light 16; Gary Milburn/First Light 20; Lynn M. Stone 22

Printed and bound in Canada

For more information on
this series and other
Whitecap Books titles,
visit our web site at
www.whitecap.ca

Canadian Cataloguing in Publication Data

Swanson, Diane, 1944–
    Welcome to the world of skunks

    Includes index.
    ISBN 1-55110-855-0

    1. Skunks—Juvenile literature. I. Title.
QL737.C25S923 1999   j599.76'8   C99-910842-5

The publisher acknowledges the support of the Canada Council for the
Arts and the Cultural Services Branch of the Government of British Columbia
for our publishing program. We acknowledge the financial support of the
Government of Canada through the Book Industry Development Program
for our publishing activities.

The author gratefully acknowledges the support of the British Columbia
Arts Council.

Contents

World of Difference

SPRAYING STINKY PERFUME HAS MADE SKUNKS FAMOUS. It's what they do to protect themselves from danger. But skunks don't spray often; in fact, some never do. They're normally quiet-living animals that try to avoid trouble.

A member of the weasel family, skunks have shiny, thick coats—usually black with white markings. A layer of short, wavy fur helps keep them warm, and a layer of long, straight hair helps keep them dry.

Four main kinds of skunks live in North America. Striped skunks usually have stripes—though some have none at all.

Bright eyes and a furry coat make the striped skunk a handsome creature.

1

The little spotted skunk often builds nests of grass or hay.

Spotted skunks are spotted, but they also have broken stripes down their backs. As you might guess, hog-nosed skunks have hoglike noses for poking into the dirt. And hooded skunks have long white hair that spreads out—like a hood—across their head and neck.

The smallest skunks are the spotted, but

even the biggest—striped and hog-nosed skunks—are only the size of pet cats. Most skunks have long tails, especially the hooded, which have tails that are longer than their bodies.

Strong, curved claws on a skunk's front feet make great digging tools. But spotted skunks put their claws to a special use. They can climb trees to escape danger and find food.

Most skunks tend to stay out of the water, but they can swim if they have to.

SURPRISING SKUNKS

Skunks often surprise people. Here are just a few of the things they do:

- Before eating a fuzzy caterpillar, a skunk may push it around to remove the hair.
- A skunk might roll up a strip of lawn and dig for insects in the soil beneath.
- Skunks sometimes treat a car like any other enemy: they spray it.
- Striped skunks can swim for more than seven hours at a time.

3

Where in the World

A gap in an old tree trunk can make a cozy home for any skunk.

SKUNKS AREN'T FUSSY. They adopt dens near mountaintops and dens at sea level. They settle into deserts, rocky slopes, and shady woods. Wherever skunks live, they stay close to cover, such as tall grass and drainage ditches.

During the summer, skunks mostly use dens above ground. They choose ones that protect them from bad weather and from enemies, such as coyotes and owls. Hollow trees, hay piles, and barns are some of the spots they use.

Where there are cold winters, skunks often move into underground burrows.

5

They dig their own or use holes dug by other animals. The skunks line these burrows with grass and leaves and make sure there are two to five hidden "doorways." Then they can come and go safely.

Sometimes skunks share their burrows with up to 24 others. These roommates might include different kinds of animals, such

The hooded skunk lives in regions that have warm weather most of the year.

as raccoons and rabbits. Sharing dens is more common during bitter weather when it helps keep the animals warm. Skunks sleep through much of the winter, waking only now and then.

Striped skunks live in Canada and the United States, while spotted skunks also live in Mexico and Central America. Hooded and hog-nosed skunks find homes in the southern United States, Mexico, and Central America. The hog-nosed live in South America as well.

SKUNK UNDER A BUNK

Shelter in towns and campsites often attracts skunks. They walk through underground pipes, crawl beneath buildings, and settle into sheds. Some wriggle right under cots used by sleeping campers.

Where there are people, there's also food. Skunks steal corn from gardens and garbage from dumps. They even lick tossed-out food cans. One skunk got its head stuck and clattered blindly down the road before some-one yanked the can off.

7

World Full of Food

ON SUNNY DAYS, SKUNKS RARELY EAT. They do most of their hunting in the dark of night. Still, hunger can drive skunks—especially the spotted kind—to look for food almost any time.

Skunks usually hunt close to home. Their short legs and flat feet aren't built for traveling far. They usually just toddle along, but they can run for short stretches. Top speed for a striped skunk is about 16 kilometres (10 miles) an hour. Spotted skunks can run faster.

Insects such as beetles, grasshoppers, and crickets make up many meals for a

A Canada goose tries to keep this skunk from having eggs for supper.

Dinner for two!
These little skunks
are sniffing out a
meal of insects.

skunk. It pounces on some and digs others right out of the ground. Sometimes it slashes a wasp nest with its sharp claws, then catches the insects as they charge out. Stinging wasps don't usually harm the skunk. It kills them by rolling them between its thick-skinned front paws.

Skunks, particularly spotted skunks, also

eat other kinds of food. They hunt for bird eggs, worms, snails, clams, frogs, mice, lizards, and young rabbits. And they eat "salads" of fresh grass, leaves, fruit, and nuts when they're in season.

A skunk can hear better than it can see, but its sense of smell works best of all. The striped skunk can sniff out insects even when they're underground. As it waddles about, it stops often to smell for food. It also sneezes a lot, which helps clear its nose and make smelling easier.

Alien Skunks

Skunks that move in where they don't belong can cause trouble. On one island—where no skunks had ever lived—pet skunks escaped from their owners. Living in the wild, they gobbled up many of the eggs that quails lay in ground nests. They ate plenty of the mouselike voles that barn owls feed on.

When the skunks had families, the trouble got worse. The aliens made it harder for quails, barn owls, and other wildlife to survive.

11

World of Words

SKUNKS NOT ONLY TELL, THEY SHOW. They squeal if they're hurt, and hiss if they're mad. Sometimes, they grunt, growl, or snarl, especially when they're young kits. But if danger threatens, skunks let their bodies do most of the talking— without making a sound.

To start with, a skunk's black-and-white color is a warning to other animals. It's like a flag that means, "Watch out!" An enemy, such as a wolf or a cat, might respect that warning and decide not to attack. But if it moves closer, the skunk starts talking in several other ways.

H-i-s-s-s. Gr-r-ow-l. An angry skunk makes angry noises.

13

Looking its enemy in the eye, the skunk tries to make itself look much bigger—and scarier—than it really is. It arches its back and holds up its tail. And the long hairs on the tail stand right on end.

If that doesn't make the intruder leave, the skunk might shuffle backward, then waddle stiffly forward. It might hiss and

Tail raised and hair fluffed, a skunk seems larger than life.

click its teeth, and stamp its front feet on the ground.

Some skunks, especially the spotted skunks, might do a handstand, which makes them look much taller and more frightening. Then they walk on their front feet with their tails held high in the air. Spotted skunks can often walk this way for several metres (many feet).

The final warning is a serious threat. A skunk points its back end at the enemy, which means, "Go—or else I'll shoot!"

No Time, No Warning

In an emergency, skunks might not have time to give any warnings. One night, a skunk discovered a sleeping bag at a campsite. It stopped to rest, curling up on the bag—and waking the person sleeping inside.

The shocked camper grabbed the skunk and threw it into the air. It landed on all four feet, unhurt. But it was so startled that it fired out a stream of smelly oil. The camper didn't have time to escape from his sleeping bag.

Smelly World

SKUNKS HATE THE SMELL OF SKUNK OIL. They try not to get any of it on themselves—or on other skunks. If there's a chance the wind could blow the oil their way, they might decide not to spray at all.

A pair of small glands produces the stinky, white or yellowish oil. When the skunk fires, it squeezes muscles that force the oil through two nipples at its back end. It can fire with one nipple or the other, or use them both at the same time. And it can shoot the oil as a fine spray or as a stream of rain-sized drops.

Skunks don't fire blindly. Most of them

Faced with an enemy that won't leave, a skunk might have to make a stink.

17

curve their bodies around so that their eyes and their back ends both focus on the target. Spotted skunks can spray while doing a handstand and arching their backs. That way it's easier for them to fire at the faces of taller enemies.

Most skunks can strike their targets from up to 5 metres (16 feet) away. Their aim is more

A skunk shoots from the rear. Its spraying gear is at its back end.

accurate for distances that are under 3 metres (10 feet).

Each jet of spray contains less than 3 millilitres (about half a teaspoon) of oil. A skunk can usually fire up to eight shots, then its glands need a couple of days to build up a full supply again.

The smell of skunk oil is enough to make animals—and people—feel sick. What's worse, the oil can sting the skin and eyes. There's no lasting damage, but most animals learn to leave skunks well alone.

SMELLING THE FIRE ALARM

Skunk smells can save lives. Many large underground mines depend on strong odors to warn miners of danger such as fire. It's hard to warn them with sound. The machines they use are very noisy.

Mines mix chemicals that make a smell like skunk oil. In emergencies, they drop some into the air-conditioning system. The smell travels through the mine in a flash. And the miners stop what they're doing and rush to safety.

19

New World

KITS COULDN'T SURVIVE WITHOUT THEIR MOTHER. Yet she gets no help from their father. In fact, he never even sees the kits.

Before they are born, a mother skunk finds a safe place for them to live—usually in an underground burrow. One hog-nosed skunk made a nest for her kits on a pile of grass inside an old mine.

Skunk families often arrive in May and come in different sizes. Striped skunks usually give birth to five to seven kits at once, while hog-nosed skunks give birth to one to four. Some skunks have just one

As a spotted kit grows its first coat, furry white dots appear on its face.

21

Two striped kits check out a log not far from their burrow.

family a year, but striped and spotted skunks may have two.

Kits are helpless at birth. They can't hear much, and their eyes are shut. Many weigh only as much as 10 marshmallows. Their tiny, wrinkled bodies barely have any fur, though a black-and-white pattern already shows on their pinkish skin.

If they have to move, their mother uses her teeth to pick the kits up by the loose skin on the backs of their necks. Mostly, they just snuggle close to her to keep warm and safe. The milk mom provides helps them grow bigger and stronger.

By the time they're two to four weeks old, the kits are wearing furry coats, and they can open their eyes. At six weeks, they're scrambling around their burrow, playing. The kits are ready to head out of their den to explore a much bigger world.

FIRST TIME OUT

It was getting dark when five striped skunk kits squirmed out of a hollow tree. They were off on their very first walk! Tails held high, they followed their mother through the woods—one after the other. When she stopped and sniffed, they stopped and sniffed. When she dug up beetles, they dug up beetles.

By the time they circled back home, the kits were all tired out. The sun was rising, and it was soon time to sleep.

Small World

LITTLE SKUNKS MAKE MIDNIGHT MEALS FOR BIG OWLS. Bobcats and dogs sometimes attack them, too. That's why a mother skunk doesn't let her kits wander around alone. She keeps them close and tries to sense any danger.

As the kits grow, their mother also keeps busy getting enough food for them. They stop feeding on her milk when they're about two months old. But they're not picky eaters. They gobble up whatever food their mother can find for them.

Bit by bit, they learn how to get their own meals. They hunt as a family, copying

Awake and ready for action, these young skunks peek out of their den.

25

what their mother does. The kits learn to graze on grass and nibble berries. They practice digging up worms and pouncing on insects and mice.

When they head to a stream to drink, the kits watch their mother catch small fish with her paws. The first time they try it, they usually just splash around. But that can be fun. Kits splash

"Hmm, might be something down there to eat," this kit seems to be thinking.

one another in play. Sometimes they also pretend to fight—even stamping their feet as if they were warning an enemy to go away.

When it's time for the family to move on, the mother skunk might whistle softly. That's her way of saying, "Line up, everyone."

Before the summer ends, the kits are usually as big as their mother. They have learned to feed and protect themselves. In the fall, they head off to live on their own—for up to 10 years.

SPOTTING SPOTTED SKUNKS

Read the signs and you'll know if spotted skunks are around. They drop their stools, called scats, almost everywhere. They also spread a musky odor about. As they squeeze through den openings and holes in buildings, they often leave hairs behind. And in snow and mud, they make tracks that show the long claws on their front feet. When skunks walk slowly, they place their back feet in the prints just made by their front feet.

Index